A HUNDRED YEARS OF SAIL

A
HUNDRED YEARS
OF SAIL

Beken of Cowes

COLLINS
St James's Place, London
1981

William Collins Sons & Co Ltd
London · Glasgow · Sydney · Auckland
Toronto · Johannesburg

First published in Great Britain 1981
© Beken of Cowes Ltd

Introduction © Hammond Innes —
William Collins, Publishers, London 1981

ISBN 0 00 216811 1

Photoset in Bembo

Made and printed in Great Britain by
Balding + Mansell, Wisbech

CONTENTS

Foreword
by HRH Prince Philip, Duke of Edinburgh

Introduction
by Hammond Innes

The Tools of the Trade
by Kenneth Beken

Photographic Index and Captions

Some people are said to have an eye for a horse; the Bekens have a lens for a yacht. The difference is that this book allows everyone to share the results of their talents.

I have been going to Cowes fairly regularly for more than 30 years and although I have a quite unjustified reputation for impatience with photographers I can say that, far from being irritated by the attentions of first Keith, and more recently Kenneth, Beken, I have always been rather flattered to see them aiming in my direction. For one thing, they know what yacht racing is all about, and they never get in the way.

Beken addicts will love this book. Many others cannot fail to be impressed, and surely even the most confirmed landlubber will admit that the pictures are pretty good.

INTRODUCTION

THIS IS a sailing man's dream of a book – mine anyway. And not just because it spans a hundred years of the finest in racing yachts. Artistically it is unique, a photographic collection that has no equal. There were other photographers, of course, throughout most of those hundred years, but the parade of yachts sailing through the pages of this book is the photographic work of one family, the Bekens – four generations of them; Alfred Edward, Frank, Keith and Kenneth, each photographer's son learning as constant companion and assistant from his father.

There is thus a remarkable artistic continuity in these photographs, even to the present day when cameras are so much lighter and easier to handle and professionals think nothing of using half-a-dozen or more rolls of film to get a single picture. The Bekens, however, still think of themselves as being in the business of 'maritime portrait photography', regarding the sea as their studio, the posing of the subject to be arranged either with the co-operation of the ship's skipper or the manoeuvring of the Beken launch. Though using the most up-to-date Hasselblad camera, it is seldom that more than half-a-dozen shots are taken.

I wonder if those of us who have been fortunate enough to possess a Beken calendar have ever considered the problem of choosing the year's twelve pictures. We all have cameras, we all have pictures piled in drawers, crammed into folders, some of us even file them carefully. But even so, to keep track of them, to pick a hundred or so for an illustrated talk, and then, most difficult of all, ensure that each picture gets back into its proper place . . . I have despaired at times. So what about the Bekens, with their four generations of pictures?

They have approximately seventy-five thousand black and white plates, the older ones requiring care and maintenance to preserve them. That's the sum total of a century of black and white photography. The colour pictures are more recent, of course. There are some twenty-seven thousand of them, built up over a period of fifteen years. That's more than a hundred thousand pictures from which to pick just twelve for the calendar months.

It sounds incredible for a professional firm of photographers, but they have only recently completed a card index system for the black and white pictures. It took them five years, Keith Beken and his son Kenneth making all the decisions – that is, choosing the one, or at most two, shots that should be included in the file – with the aid of perhaps one trusted member of the staff of six.

Kenneth Beken said to me recently, 'We've stayed with portraits of yachts, so you can always tell a Beken photograph.' We were standing in his home on the waterfront at Cowes looking down on the Beken launch and the little cat he uses for sailing. The water out there in the Solent is a way of life to him, both work and play. Unlike his brother, who is an engineer and diver, he never seems to have wanted to do anything else since he began to get the feel of it, out in the launch when he was in the carry-cot stage.

He is the fourth generation of a business that started as a hobby with Alfred Edward Beken. The first pictures in this book are by Alfred Edward himself. The state of the plates has necessitated some retouching, but even so these pictures rank with some of the best of the professional yacht photographers of the period. And yet he always regarded himself as an amateur. He had a chemist's shop in Canterbury and his yacht photography led him in 1888 to move to Cowes. But he still regarded himself as an amateur, even after he began selling prints of his yacht pictures at a penny a time. That was in 1894, which properly marks the start of the thriving prints business the Bekens have developed from their shop in Cowes. He was also accepting the occasional commission, one of which was from Osborne House to record the passing over the water of the dead Queen Victoria in 1901.

But it was his son, Frank Beken, who really launched Beken of Cowes as professionals in yacht portraiture. And not just yachts – all manner of ships, naval as well as the great White Stars and Cunarders. He was out in the Solent when *Olympic* and HMS *Hawke* were in collision and gave evidence in support of the captain of the *Olympic*. The White Star Line did not win at the Enquiry, but they promoted their captain to the *Titanic*, and as he steamed out from Southampton water on that terrible maiden voyage he saw the lonely figure of Frank Beken out in his boat and gave him a special blast on the siren. Beken had only two plates left. With these he took a picture of the *Titanic* approaching and another of the *Titanic* going away. I have a print of the latter, the last, the very last recorded sight of that sunk 'unsinkable'.

Frank Beken I rank with that extraordinary adventure-photographer, Cherry Kearton. Kearton, the first to photograph every species of bird in the British Isles, the first to film animals in the wild, who could write in 1935 that he had spent the 'best part of forty-four years in photographing wild animals in four out of five continents', referred to three characteristics required of a photographer using the open air as his studio: 'Inventiveness, a love of the open country, and a curiosity concerning wild creatures'.

These three precepts are exactly applicable to the work of Frank Beken if they are changed to read: Inventiveness, a love of the sea, and a curiosity about ships (particularly sailing ships).

Inventiveness he certainly had, for the problem in the first place was a technical one. This is covered in detail by Kenneth Beken in a note preceding the pictures. I see it as a problem of seamanship, too, which only a man who loved the sea could have solved. To design a faster shutter is one thing, but then to go for a big, heavy box of a camera, gimbal it with both arms, using just his legs to balance himself in a small boat and activating the shutter by a rubber bulb clamped between his teeth, only a man of the utmost determination in the pursuit of something to which he is dedicated would do that. And then to position himself firmly in the path of a racing machine of two to four hundred tons, powered by some twelve thousand square feet of canvas carried on solid wooden masts up to one hundred and fifty feet tall . . .

A modern Beken photograph is, relatively, a much simpler operation; out in the high-speed launch, position either yacht or launch as necessary, using the natural studio lighting to the best advantage, then take the portraits – five or six or eight, whatever is required, re-positioning the launch for each shot. But when Frank Beken started taking pictures with his Mark I camera he had no launch, only an eighteen foot clinker-built dinghy which he rowed out and positioned himself.

So, when you are examining the early pictures, looking at them either with a yachtsman's appreciation of the nature of the boat or purely as marine examples of photographic art, just imagine yourself for a moment behind the lens of the camera, actually taking the picture. The camera is heavy. I have held it myself, and I have had it weighed – exactly five kilograms! You are using plates. No time to re-load. It is *Brynhild*, say, and she is racing. You see her coming up over the horizon five miles away, and you have just this one chance. Everything must be right – the light, the shutter speed, the focus, and most important of all, the framing of the picture, so that the length of the yacht and the top of her mast are all there, the light catching the sails, the bow wave expressive of her speed . . . everything, please God, everything absolutely right. The one take, no second chance, and the whole operation dependent on that first positioning of the dinghy. And always the risk that some switch of the wind, or a wild gust taking the helmsman by surprise, may send that mad, towering, canvas-piled monster thundering down on you.

Viewed like that it will be seen that Frank Beken in his tiny boat faced much the same problems and dangers photographing yachts in the Solent that Kearton faced recording the wild life of four continents. That is why I bracket these two very individual cameramen together as they worked in their own particular fields around the turn of the century. But there is one very marked difference. In the case of Beken a son has always followed the father. It is this continuity which makes the quality, and the spread, of this book a unique photographic record.

HAMMOND INNES

Frank Beken with his camera

THE TOOLS OF THE TRADE

EVEN AS the Old Masters had to make their own brushes and paints, so the first Bekens had to devise, experiment with and construct the equipment they used in the early days of their photography.

Frank Beken started his photography at the age of eight in 1888 having learned from his father Alfred. When he was only fourteen his pictures were being sold professionally. They were taken on a box camera of wood and canvas which produced a negative of up to 12 × 10 inches. This model proved impractical at sea where sea water caused rapid deterioration and in 1897 the Bekens devised a camera to their own specifications. This proved so successful that it was the basis for all subsequent models to 1970. It comprised a mahogany box with an 8 × 6 inch glass plate at one end and a movable lens and shutter at the other. On top was a smaller wooden box with a lens and ground glass screen to act as viewfinder while the shutter was fired by biting on a rubber ball making a noise akin to the sound of the starting gun. The Beken ingenuity did not rest there and enlargements were made on an apparatus made from wood and parts of an old bicycle with daylight providing the light source.

In recent years the increasing speed of yachts and motor boats has meant the basic Beken camera has been too slow to handle and the number of photographs limited by the weight of the dark slides used to hold the glass negatives. Keith Beken chose a Swedish Hasselblad camera. It is versatile and robust and takes a $2\frac{1}{4}$ inch square (6 × 6 cm) negative. He uses a standard (80 mm) lens and Ilford's FP4 (125 ASA) black and white film or Kodak Ektachrome colour film (64 ASA). Sea water is still a problem in maintaining the camera in good condition and after a full day at sea the camera has to be stripped down and all the salt water washed off.

As the Beken camera has become more sophisticated to keep pace with the development of yachts so has the Beken craft. From Frank's wooden dinghy to the motor launch he commissioned after the First World War through to the 1971 Boston Whaler capable of over thirty knots, the Bekens have always had craft which they could manoeuvre to catch yachts at their best angle. A perfect understanding of sailing and sail boats has been an essential factor in the family's success whether photographing from their own launch in the Solent or from a helicopter in Hawaii.

I

II

III

IV

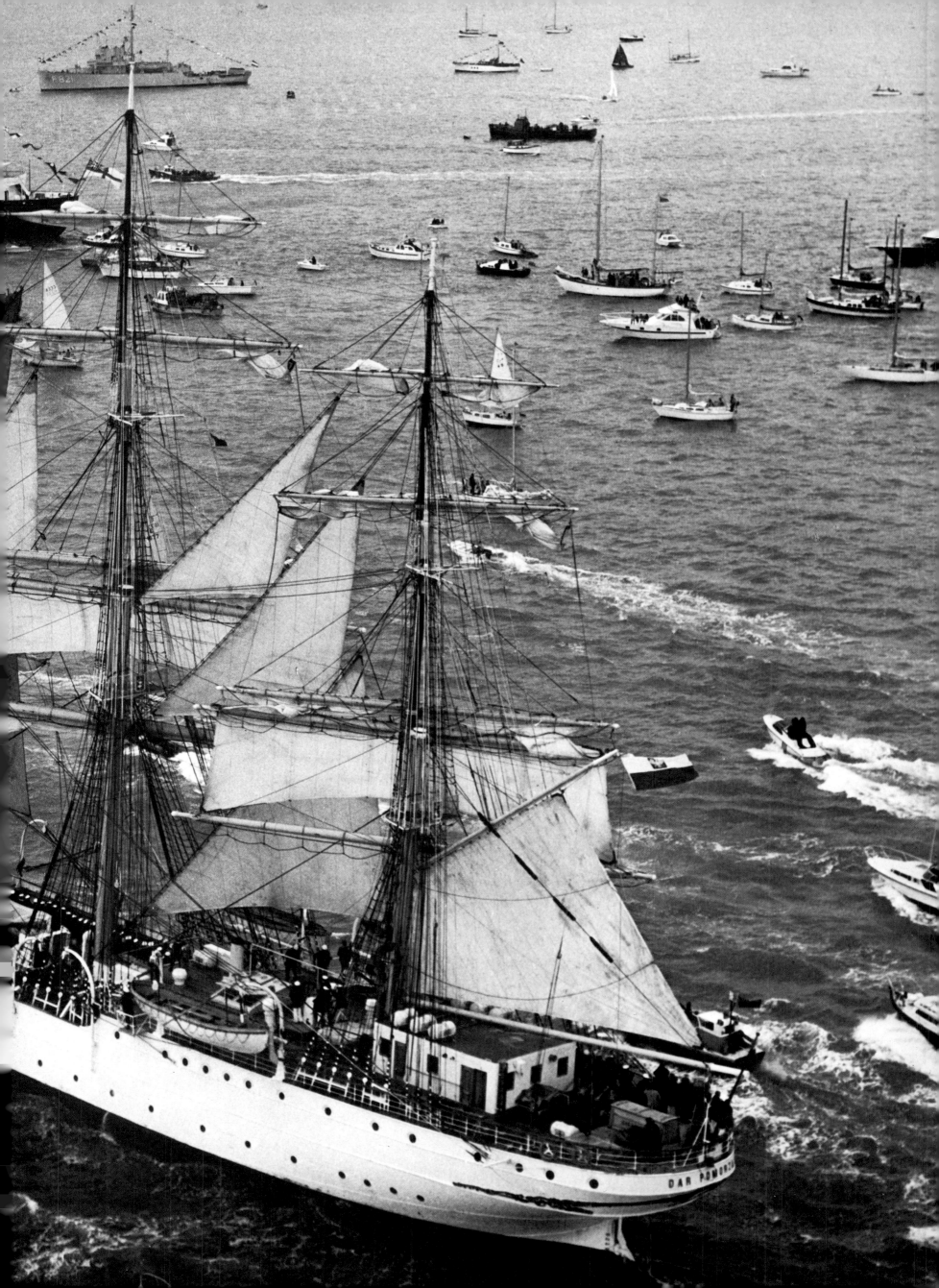

PHOTOGRAPHIC INDEX
AND CAPTIONS

PART ONE

WE HAVE SEEN what may be called the era of the glory of sail, the magnificent schooners, the great cutters and the big ketches and yawls. All over 100 feet in length and anything between 200 and 400 tons. On studying these yachts one is struck by their size, compared with the helmsman at his tiller or wheel. Every one looks a 'yacht' in the truest sense of the word – graceful, elegant, purposeful, majestic. Their canvas, of best Egyptian cotton, sets without a wrinkle, their spars (masts, booms) are made of whole trees, their area of sail colossal, their main booms trespassing far over the stern, great coils of manila sheeting all handed without winches. The racing was keen and not without accident. In 1894 *Satanita* rammed *Valkyrie II* just forward of the mast, and cut her to the waterline whereupon she sank – 400 tons and 127 feet in length travelling at ten knots cutting *Valkyrie* to the bone . . . .

In 1896 another catastrophe occurred. In the words of a witness '*Isolde* slewed across *Meteor's* bows and her bowsprit was broken. *Meteor* (400 tons) went ahead, her mainboom raked *Isolde*'s deck from stem to stern: all the crew leapt overboard to save their lives with the exception of Baron von Zedwitz, the owner, who was caught by the falling boom; on being taken to hospital, he expired.'

In 1893 *Britannia* had been designed and built for Edward, Prince of Wales, and this period of yachting owed a great debt to Royal patronage. King Edward VII, the German Emperor Wilhelm II and King Alphonse XIII were all enthusiasts and contributed heavily both in yachts and prizes.

The First World War in 1914 stopped all sailing for pleasure and it was not to be revived again for many years; finance and good seamen being a premium. In the next pages, we shall see the gradual change to 'Bermudian rig', the J-class with their 'Marconi' masts slowly changing to the new rig and the newer yachts being built to that rig. All sails were still made of Egyptian cotton, and the design of spinnakers was changing, not always for the better.

The change to Bermuda rig took place around 1920 and it is in this era that the 12 metres and 8 metres designs will be seen to come into their own. In 1925, the first Fastnet race took place, bringing to our pages yachts of a smaller dimension but seaworthy both as racing and cruising yachts. The magnificent J-class were still the 'greyhounds of the sea' and of course as challengers for the America's Cup, before the advent of the Second World War in 1939.

BLOODHOUND (1880)
No B191/G 12″ × 10″ plate 1/125th at f10

Bloodhound was designed and built for the Marquis of Ailsa by William Fife Jnr in 1874. She was a beautiful representative of the forty-tonners and began winning races virtually from the day she was launched. These yachts were known for their grace and sea-keeping qualities. They were extremely strong and could race in winds that would lift the mast out of most modern craft. The successes and history of this yacht would fill a book; she was once sunk on the start line by a steam yacht but was salvaged and repaired to race again another day! In 217 races she received 143 prizes until she was burnt out whilst at Southampton in 1922. Her mast is exhibited at the Royal Yacht Squadron in Cowes, as the main flagstaff.

IREX (1884)
No 58 12″ × 10″ plate 1/150th at f11

With five of her crew on the bowsprit, ready to set her flying jib after rounding a mark, *Irex* tramps on to win her nineteenth race in her first season. Designed with a straight stem and great jackyard topsail by A. Richardson for John Jameson, she was launched in 1884 and is everybody's idea of the classical yacht of the 1880s. These yachts were built to last for more than a generation with solid oak booms and bowsprits made from one tree-trunk. Note the length of her spinnaker pole just showing above the cross-trees.

JULLANAR (1893)
No 8487 12″ × 10″ plate 1/125th at f10

Jullanar was launched in 1875 and immediately proved successful. She was a breakthrough in design by E. H. Benthell and built on the east coast of England. This 126-ton yawl was designed to have the longest waterline compared with the smallest

frictional surface and shortest heel that it was possible to unite in the same hull. She represented the first breakaway from the smaller naval vessels with her clipper bow and canoe stern, and she was regarded as being rather ugly in her day. She was at her best in strong winds and a good all-rounder in most weather conditions. When this photograph was taken, nearly twenty years after her launch, she was still well up in the Yawl Class races.

LITTLE RONA (1905)
No 7 Half plate 1 second at f8

A quiet study of a fine ocean-going barque idling at anchor in the river Medina at Cowes. In the transitionary period from sail to power these ships would fuel up with coal at the deep water wharves whilst their owners would entertain at the exclusive yacht clubs. The crew is just putting the finishing touches to the fresh paintwork with the greatest care being taken over the figurehead which was always gaily decorated. Her flying jibs are set to dry, and the whole atmosphere is one of gentle stillness.

THISTLE (1890)
No 8011 12″ × 10″ plate 1/150th at f11

Designed for a Mr Bell by G. L. Watson. *Thistle* was to be the Scottish challenger for the America's Cup in 1887. However, racing against *Volunteer* she lost two out of the three races and returned beaten. As a 139-rater she collected twenty-two trophies in her first year, but had proved hard to sail to windward, the main reason being that her keel was not deep enough. She was later bought by the Kaiser and formed the first of his fleet of *Meteors*. She was rerigged but still retained her attractive lines and fine clipper bow.

HMS *VICTORY* and *MISTLETOE* (1882)
No 5003 12″ × 10″ plate 1/150th at f10

A splendid historical photograph. HMS *Victory* is in the background, whilst in the foreground a 'sale of effects' is being held on *Mistletoe* in Portsmouth Harbour. *Victory* was built in six years by Chatham Docks and launched on 7 May 1765 with forty-eight officers and 771 crew. She was a 104-gun ship of the line, 186 feet long with a beam of fifty-two feet. She was Nelson's flagship in the last major engagement of sailing warships at Trafalgar. (11.40 am, 21 October 1805). She is now preserved in Portsmouth Naval Dockyard. Ships of *Victory*'s type could only sail up to seventy degrees to the wind compared with today's thirty-eight degrees of the ocean-racers.

MINOTAUR (23 June 1887)
No 110 Half plate 1/200th at f8

Minotaur was built from 1861 and launched in 1863 at the Milwall Shipping Co. in London. She was 400 feet long with a beam of fifty-nine feet, and with a full load she drew twenty-seven feet. Displacing 10,690 tons she could approach fifteen knots under power. She was armed with four nine-inch guns and twenty-four seven-inch guns and carried 705 men. When launched she carried five masts but could only reach nine and a half knots, so two masts were removed in 1887. She served as the flagship of the Channel Squadron for eighteen years and in 1885 was fitted with the first searchlight and torpedo tubes. This photograph shows her during the fleet review by Queen Victoria on 23 June 1887. *Minotaur* was later converted for training use and was eventually broken up in 1922 after nearly sixty years afloat.

TALISMAN (1888)
No B/1/A Half plate 1/200th at f8

A quiet Sunday and time off for the dock loaders at the Cowes quay, the railway lines quiet and the cranes stowed. *Talisman* was one of the working barquentines that kept the Cowes shops well stocked in the summer season, and each crew was very proud of its particular ship and would ensure she always looked her best. Here, though, they are eyeing a steam yacht alongside bunkering up with coal. Perhaps they realise that this could be the start of a new era of power, that sailing cargo ships are doomed. One is puzzled by the curious windmill on board *Talisman*; could it be a pump for water or ventilation?

VALKYRIE I (1891)
No 8065 12″ × 10″ plate 1/150th at f11

The first of a series of fine yachts to bear this name, *Valkyrie I* was built in 1889 ostensibly to challenge for the America's Cup. However, due to an impasse between the New York Yacht Club and the Royal Yacht Squadron about the declaration of the challengers' measurements, the event never took place. In her first year she won twenty-three cups in thirty-three starts. She was classed as a 77-rater of ninety-four tons designed by G. L. Watson and built in Southampton. Her clipper bow, long bowsprit and overhanging boom make her look much longer than her eighty-five feet. She excelled in strong winds but could not match the performance of others in light airs and was replaced by *Valkyrie II* in 1893. Note the mastheadman half-way up the rigging (to clear the foresails during tacking) and the long tiller used for steering.

GALATEA (1886)
No 7372 12″ × 10″ plate Open flash approx 15 secs at f8

It is incredible to think that this picture shows the interior of an America's Cup yacht and not of a Victorian mansion! *Galatea* was owned and raced by Lt W. Henn and challenged in 1886 against the American *Mayflower*. This saloon was encompassed by a ninety-ton racing cutter of 103 feet and a fifteen-foot beam. One can imagine her crew busy stowing all those ornaments and rolling up the carpets before each race and remembering to douse the fire! *Galatea* had one unusual permanent crew member – a pet monkey called Peggy – who would run up and down the bowsprit shouting encouragement when the yacht was in the lead.

ATTEMPT (1893)
No 8480 12″ × 10″ plate 1/200th at f8

The Prince of Wales has arrived with his new cutter *Britannia*, and all eyes are on Cowes. The *Attempt* was a working barge, based in Cowes, that sailed round the south coast of England collecting and delivering cargoes at all the ports on her route. With a crew of two – and the ever present dog – she was a regular sight, especially during Cowes Week when the town consumed vast amounts of food and drink, from the bread and beer of the crews to the champagne and caviar of the titled.

WHITE HEATHER (1896)
No 7 Half plate 1/4th at f8

White Heather was typical of the steam yachts that came to Cowes at the turn of the century. Generally powered by triple expansion engines, some still carried sail for gentle cruising. These yachts were decorated below decks with the best furnishings and carpentry in a grand Victorian style, and to be invited aboard was regarded as a great honour. Gallons of fresh cream and cases of strawberries were loaded by tenders each morning for the afternoon parties and after the day's racing the yachts came alive with assembled dignitaries. Here, *White Heather* is moored off the coal quay awaiting the tide enabling her to come alongside. The picture is set off nicely by the local boys digging for fish bait before the tide covers the flats.

VALKYRIE II (1893)
No 8460 12″ × 10″ plate 1/150th at f10

Valkyrie II was built side by side with the great *Britannia* in the D. & W. Henderson yard on the Clyde. Designed by G. L. Watson, she was the challenger for the 1893 America's Cup. Only a little smaller than *Britannia*, they would race in close company with her other contemporaries – sometimes too close. They had at least two collisions, in one case having to cut away *Britannia*'s bowsprit in the English Channel! *Valkyrie* lost the America's Cup to *Vigilant* in 1893, but accepted a challenge to race on the Clyde the next year. It was whilst tuning up for this race that a fatal accident occurred. *Satanita* on starboard was approaching the line but found a smaller yacht on collision course. In avoiding this yacht, she rammed *Valkyrie* amidships, both yachts then striking a steam yacht. One man was killed and *Valkyrie II* sank in fourteen fathoms of water. Her measurements were ninety-seven feet with a beam of twenty-one feet, and she displaced 191 tons.

VIGILANT (1894)
No 8590 12″ × 10″ plate 1/4th at f4

Vigilant was the successful defender of the America's Cup in 1893 against *Valkyrie II*. In 1894 she came to Britain for a season's racing. She was designed by Nat Herreshoff and constructed with steel topsides and a bronze bottom. She was also a centreboarder, a design which worked well in America but caused constant trouble in Britain where she kept running aground and on one occasion, the centreboard fell out altogether! She was beaten overall in the season by *Britannia*, and it is a pity that the Prince of Wales never had a crack at the 'Auld Mug'. *Vigilant* was 128 feet overall with a waterline of eighty-six feet. She had a beam of twenty-six feet, a sail area of 11,600 square feet and displaced 144 tons.

COWES REGATTA (August 1894)
No PV/33 Half plate 1/200th at f8

The year is 1894 and with Queen Victoria at Osborne House, Cowes was like a second court. The Prince of Wales was probably aboard *Britannia* racing against the other huge cutters, and the crowned heads of Europe would either be racing or entertaining on their yachts moored in the harbour. Here the ladies and gentlemen are strolling along Cowes' waterfront green during the Royal Regatta, the ladies in ankle-length dresses carrying sun shades and the men with bowlers and canes. The children, in their Sunday best, are making the most of the holiday atmosphere.

BROADGLANCE (1895)
No 924 1/125th at f8

A picture of the fairer sex at play! The lady to windward, complete with straw boater, is keeping the yacht to leeward under check. Both are on a reach to the next mark and handling their yachts like professionals, sails setting perfectly. Number 2 is a Sibbick-rater similar to one built for King George V

at the Sibbick yard in five and a half days. This picture must have said a lot for female emancipation in the days before women had the right to vote – both helmswomen are in complete control, with tillers amidships.

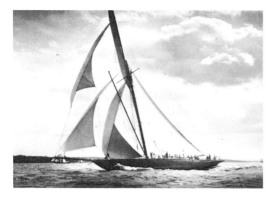

VALKYRIE III (1895)
1/125th at f10

This 1895 challenge for the America's Cup caused much friction between Britain and the New York Yacht Club. Whilst racing in the Clyde, *Valkyrie III* had proved to be a fast boat, although beaten by *Britannia* and *Ailsa*, but only in light weather and to windward. She crossed to the States, with virtually no tuning, to have three infamous races against *Defender*: in the first she maintained she was hounded by spectator craft taking her wind; in the second, again blamed on spectator craft, her boom carried away *Defender's* topmast backstay on the start line causing a protest; and the third, the Earl of Dunraven claimed that *Defender* had altered her ballast against regulations and refused to race further. She lost the protest – and the cup. The friction caused by these incidents was only cleared by the Lipton challenges. *Valkyrie III* was designed by G. L. Watson with an overall length of 100 feet and a sail area of 13,000 square feet. With such a spinnaker pole one can understand the need for so many crew to handle all that canvas.

RAISING THE TOPSAIL (1896)
1/150th at f10

The Prince of Wales steps aboard *Britannia*, and the crew is raising the topsail. In the 1880s there were no such things as winches. To raise this sail, which must have weighed tons, the crew climbed up the ratlines, crossed over to swing on the halyard, using their weight to add to the fifteen men on the deck, and hauled on the halyard at the foot of the mast. A man can be seen at the cross-trees, manhandling the sail on its way up past the jaws of the gaff, and another is at the foot of the mast feeding the sail up. It is a calm morning a good two hours before the start, which was the time taken to get everything shipshape before the first gun.

CREOLE (13 August 1892)
No B/25 12″ × 10″ plate 1/120th at f9

This attractive 40-rater was built in 1890 by Forrest & Son on the east coast of England for Col Villiers Bagot. She was designed by G. L. Watson who was famed for his larger yachts, but most people regarded this little yacht as one of his most attractive. She was seventy feet long and carried 4279 square feet of sail on a well proportioned rig. At an age when most modern boats would have retired, she was still winning races; her most notable being the Emperor's Cup in 1904. By 1906 she was racing with other handicapped yachts in one class. This class had forty-five starts in twelve weeks, quite a condensed series for such yachts compared with today. She was still racing forty years later in 1929.

NAVAHOE (1894)
No 9784 12″ × 10″ plate 1/125th at f8

Navahoe was designed and built for the American Royal Phelps Carroll by Nat Herreshoff in 1893. She was 126 feet overall with a waterline of eighty-seven feet. Her beam was twenty-four feet and she drew twelve and a half feet. She displaced 114 tons and carried a large sail area of 11,000 square feet. Against her contemporaries, she proved very fast-reaching and running; she had an epic race with *Britannia* in 1893 across the English Channel when the two boats were never more than 150 yards apart right to the finish (which *Navahoe* won on protest). Between the years 1901 and 1906 she won seventy first prizes. Here she is pictured reaching up the Solent from the west, about to set her spinnaker. The man on the bowsprit is handling the spinnaker guy.

ALL HANDS ON THE BOWSPRIT! (1897)
No 9009 12″ × 10″ plate 1/120th at f8

Twenty-four of the crew of *Meteor II* are strung out along the bowsprit to lower the bow and raise the stern of this fine yacht to move off the sandbank which has trapped her. This must have caused considerable embarrassment to her owner, His Imperial Majesty the German Emperor, no doubt his competitors on *Britannia* were shouting 'helpful' comments. Built in 1896, *Meteor* was an extremely fast yacht and won her first races in Britain.

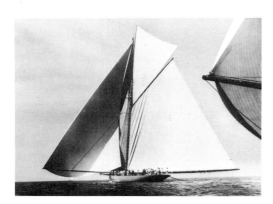

SHAMROCK (1899)
No 49 Half plate 1/150th at f10

This photograph illustrates the vast sail area that these yachts carried. *Britannia* is pressing hard and closing on *Shamrock*, and the crew has its work cut out to keep ahead. The 13,200 square feet of sail needed up to forty men. This was Sir Thomas Lipton's first yacht to challenge for the America's Cup but she was beaten in 1899 by *Columbia*. Four more *Shamrocks* were built to try to win the cup, all unsuccessfully. The last, *Shamrock V*, is still afloat having been recently reconditioned to her original J-class specification. *Shamrock I* was designed by Fife of Scotland and built by John Thorneycroft. She was 131 feet long and displaced 260 tons.

RAINBOW (1898)
No 9153 12″ × 10″ plate 1/150th at f10

Designed by G. L. Watson and built for C. L. Orr Ewing, MP by D. W. Henderson of Glasgow in 1898, *Rainbow* was a beautiful yacht. She measured 132 feet overall and carried 13,500 square feet of sail. She was built not to race but simply as a yacht. With her large sail area and her displacement of 331 tons, she proved to be quite fast as this picture shows. With her sheets eased off catching a stiff southwesterly on a reach, this schooner is certainly moving! In 1904 she was bought by a German sailing syndicate and renamed *Hamburg*.

VALHALLA (1899)
No 8793 12″ × 10″ plate 1/150th at f10

This lovely full-rigged ship of 1490 tons and 245 feet was designed by Storey and built by Ramage & Ferguson as a private yacht for Col Laycock. She later passed into the hands of Lord Crawford for world exploration voyages. Launched in 1892, she sailed round the world in 1905, during which expedition the owner made a remarkable collection of rare birds and amassed a wealth of knowledge on land and sea area which he bequeathed to oceanographers. In 1913 *Valhalla* was sold to a fishing syndicate as a cold storage vessel but was then converted for the shipment of bananas. She was wrecked off the coast of Portugal a few years later in 1922. Standard crew in her early days numbered 100. She was a fine example of a steam auxiliary and in 1905 raced against Lord Brassey's *Sunbeam* and the American schooner *Atlantic*. Her top speed under canvas was sixteen knots.

PART TWO

In 1937 J-class racing took place for the last time before the declaration of war in 1939. We have seen the last of the fine great cutters with their pencil-slim hulls and raking masts, limited in a good blow, however, when they were forced to retire.

Again due to lack of finance and good seamen, it was many years before yachting for pleasure started again. The yachts, both racing and cruising, were smaller, more efficient, all with the compact Bermudian rig. So, with the early years after the war, the hulls were still wood planked, the masts of wood, hollow or solid, and designs of hulls for ocean racers were seen rather to have copied the metre boats for speed.

Small deck winches appeared and the sheets and halyards were of manila or Italian hemp, with wire used instead on the larger yachts, and wooden dinghies and kapok life jackets were still in evidence.

Sails were of Egyptian cotton, the main boom becoming shorter, masts moving more to the centre of the yacht and thereby causing design of genoas to become bigger and mainsails smaller; in fact the rig will be seen to be inside the ends of the yacht. A typical example of this period is *Bloodhound* which, although designed in 1936, came into her own after the war with her compact yawl rig.

Although some yachts were built perhaps twenty or thirty or more years ago, modern rigs and equipment have brought them up to date with their competitors of this era. Bowsprits may have been removed, mast heels re-positioned, Bermuda masts and sails replacing the old gaff rig, giving the thirty-year-olds a new lease of life.

The day of the light displacement hull had also just begun, with high freeboard, and no overhanging ends bow or stern, long ends serving no purpose at sea in ocean-racing weather. Just five years after the war, the first reverse sheer hull was designed and five years after that a light alloy hull made its appearance named 'Gulvain'; these years were experimental and innovative.

BRYNHILD (1901)
No B58A Half plate 1/150th at f9

One of the famous series of yawls racing in the early 1900s, *Brynhild* was built in 1901 for Selwyn Calverly and later owned by Sir James Pender. Racing in this class took a dive between 1897 and 1907 when the Yacht Racing Association in Britain brought in an age allowance handicap for yachts in the 23 metre class. This meant that many smaller and older yachts could now win races against the larger yachts. Consequently many owners moved to the Mediterranean to race and it was not until 1907 when the ruling was changed that they returned. However, *Brynhild* was sunk in that year and activity in the big cutter class was quiet until its revival in the early 1930s.

COWES PARADE (August 1900)
No PV/105 Half plate 1/250th at f8

Cowes – the Mecca for yachtsmen all over the world – has not changed much since the early days of sail. The streets are still narrow and the names of the old chandlers and suppliers are still there. Here is a crowd on Cowes Parade viewing the yachts as they sail to and fro, jockeying for a good start position. The people waiting by the Squadron steps, hoping for a glimpse of visiting Royalty, are entertained by acrobats, magicians, jugglers, peddlers and buskers. In the foreground the local vicar passes the time with a parishioner and in the background a paddle steamer from Southampton arrives with its decks crowded to overflowing. The *Royal London* flagpole to the right is still there, and so is the letter box, along with the sea wall balustrade.

DISCOVERY (1901)
No 9149 12″ × 10″ plate 1/250th at f8

Built in 1899 on the Tay, *Discovery* was purpose-built for Captain Scott's expedition to the Antarctic by designer W. E. Smith, one of the chief constructors at the Admiralty. She was launched on 21 March 1901 at Dundee and became the sixth exploration vessel to bear the name *Discovery*. Made of English oak, her hull was over two feet thick and she was 171 feet overall. She was a barque-rigged auxiliary steam ship powered by a 450 bhp triple expansion steam engine. She left Cowes in 1901 for her epic voyage to the Antarctic and returned to Southsea in 1904. In 1906 she was sold to the Hudson's Bay Company for £10,000 and undertook trading voyages until 1920. In 1931 she was laid up in the East India Docks of London and in 1937 she was towed to a mooring on the Thames for public display.

CARIAD (4 August 1903)
No B114A Half plate 1/150th at f10

This lovely craft was designed by the famous A. E. Payne for Lord Dunraven and built of wood on steel frames by the Southampton yard of Somers & Payne in 1896. Of 129 tons TM she measured eighty-eight and a half feet overall with a beam of eighteen and a half feet. She was not only a racer but was designed with luxury in mind and to this day she cruises for charter in the Caribbean. This photograph shows her in her heyday during the Cowes Regatta. Her attractive bow (typically Payne) and fine counter stern, together with perfectly set canvas, show her off to perfection.

FALCON (1903)
No 102 Half plate 1/150th at f10

This shows the delightful custom of exhibiting prize flags at the end of the season's racing. These were won for first, second and third placings and were proudly flown by successful boats, a practice now sadly forgotten except by a few sentimentalists. *Falcon* was a very fast (and obviously successful) sixteen-tonner of the class known as 36-footers. She was still winning races nearly fifty years after her launch. The crew were only too pleased to be photographed as it served as a permanent record of their achievements.

SHAMROCK II (22 May 1901)
No 9427 Half plate 1/100th at f8

The second *Shamrock* was very similar to the first although designed and built by different yards. She was slightly longer at 108 feet with a tonnage of 265, but did not prove to be any faster than her predecessor. Designed by G. L. Watson, she was the longest ever challenger at 137 feet from the tip of her bowsprit to the end of her counter. *Shamrock II* was soundly beaten by *Columbia* in America and never returned to Britain. She was broken up in New York after a very short career. This picture shows a very sorry episode in May of 1901. King Edward VII was aboard as guest of the owner, Sir Thomas Lipton. One moment the yacht was creaming through the Solent, the next 110 feet of mast and 14,000 square feet of sail are over the side. Several tons of rigging, metal and canvas had to be hauled aboard before she could get a tow back to Cowes. Fortunately no one was hurt. This was not as uncommon as one might imagine in those days when the new metal masts were under trial.

CICELY (2 August 1902)
No B129/G Half plate 1/120th at f8

This beautiful schooner was designed by Fife of Scotland as a fast cruising yacht and built by Fay & Co of Southampton in 1902. Her owner, Cecil Quentin, could not resist racing her and won countless races against such yachts as *Meteor III*, *Clara* and *Nordwest*. She excelled in strong winds, particularly when close-hauled. The urgency of this fine yacht is well portrayed here, her 114 feet carrying 10,000 square feet of sail dwarfing the helmsman who is pushing her to her limits.

BONA (1903)
No 24/B2 Half plate 1/150th at f10

This elegant cutter was designed by G. L. Watson as an 83-rater of 122 tons for the Duke of Abruzzi and built by D. & W. Henderson in 1897. She is pictured

here in the conditions she liked best: light airs. In rougher weather she would lose to such racing contemporaries as *Satanita*, *Meteor* and *Rainbow*. She was steered with the aid of blocks and tackle linked to a tiller and raced under the current handicap system of the day. Owners were finding this system a little unpopular and in 1906 the Yacht Racing Association brought in the International Metre Rule which led to the larger yachts being designed to race to a fairer measurement scale. *Bona* was eighty-nine feet long with a beam of eighteen feet and her most notable achievement was in beating seventeen other starters in the Emperor's Cup of 1903.

SHAMROCK III (1903)
No 10313 Half plate 1/150th at f8

The third *Shamrock* built for Sir Thomas Lipton was launched in 1903 and challenged *Reliance* for the America's Cup that year. *Reliance* was the largest ever America's Cup yacht and naturally triumphed in the minimum of three races. *Shamrock* was a large yacht but was hopelessly outclassed. She was 134 feet long with a waterline of ninety feet, her 278 tons powered through the water by 14,154 square feet of sail. This picture captures the thrill of the moment just before her launch and her sleek Fife-designed lines can be clearly appreciated. Even twenty-six years later she was still beating younger British yachts.

SONYA, MOYANA and *BRITOMART* (August 1905)
No 108 Half plate 1/200th at f8

An early morning calm sets the scene for the start of the 52-raters. *Sonya* was a fifty-nine-foot cutter designed and built by Nat Herreshoff for the noted British helmswoman, Mrs Turner-Farley. The canvas here is just too heavy to fill, in the light air. The other two boats are slightly longer but come within the fifty-two feet rating. They were designed by A. Mylne but did not prove as fast as *Sonya* or the older *Creole*. What a quiet and tranquil study this is – even if the weather was very frustrating for the skippers and crew!

NAVAHOE and *CARIAD* (1906)
No B/108 Half plate 1/150th at f8

By this year most of the giant cutters had added a mizzen mast to help their time handicap rating and here we see the older American *Navahoe* of 114 tons in company with the British *Cariad*. Both were very fast, even with their altered split rig and our picture shows them having just rounded the mark and setting their spinnakers. Two other yachts are still beating up to the buoy and although *Cariad* is slightly ahead, *Navahoe* has the better position to windward. By the end of this season *Navahoe* had collected seventy firsts after six years' racing. Crews numbered around twenty in light conditions and with this number on board they could be handled like dinghies changing sails on rounding the marks with sheer muscle power!

SATANITA (7 August 1906)
B18/4 Half plate 1/150th at f10

Built in 1893, a classic year for these huge cutters, *Satanita* was originally equipped with a single mast and only later changed to a yawl. She set a number of records in her time. Designed by Soper she carried a mainsail of nearly 5000 square feet on the longest boom ever fitted to a British yacht – ninety-two feet. Displacing 130 tons (400 tons TM) she was certainly a powerful machine, once covering nearly 300 miles in twenty hours – an average of fifteen knots. She also set a speed record for a single-masted monohull of seventeen knots on the Clyde. It was there that she rammed *Valkyrie II* and sank her on the start line of a race in the regatta of 5 July 1894. In 1909 she was sold and went to the Mediterranean where she had a number of owners, amongst them Errol Flynn.

KARIAD (10 August 1906)
No B/108 Half plate 1/180th at f9

Kariad was designed by G. L. Watson as a single-masted cutter for Kenneth Clark in 1901. She rated as a 93-footer but was purchased by Sir James Pender who converted her to a yawl to help her handicap rating. These were the days when Cowes could boast many such fashionable yachts in a season of racing. Few owners actually raced them themselves, but would hire professional skippers and crew. So important was success in these races that when *Kariad* was soundly trounced in 1906 by such yachts as *Nyria* and *White Heather* she was taken to the breakers' yard.

ADELA (1908)
No B/113 Half plate 1/200th at f10

Adela, with her clipper bow and lovely taffrail stern, shows her paces in a good breeze during the Cowes regatta. Notice the helmsman with one hand on the wheel spokes and his other languidly at his side proving how well balanced *Adela* was. 224 tons TM and 109 feet overall she was designed by W. C. Storey in 1903 for Claud Cayley and built in Southampton. She raced against the other big schooners of her day including the Kaiser's *Meteor*, *Cetonia* and *Germania*, and now after over seventy years and a long extensive refit, she is afloat in her original splendour under the name *Heartsease*, though without the prospect of racing again.

GERMANIA (1908)
No B129/K3 Half plate 1/150th at f10

Germania close-hauled under every stitch of canvas she can carry showing her power at 122 feet overall and 366 tons TM. She was designed by German Max Oertz for Dr Krupp von Bohlen who built her in his yard, the Krupp Germania Werft, in 1903. In the big schooner fleet, she was second in size only to the Kaiser's *Meteor* of 412 tons. *Germania* was in fact faster and collected a multitude of trophies in international races before friendly rivalry became a serious business in 1914, and raced alongside such classic schooners as *Cetonia*, *Adela*, *Susanne* and *Cicely*. How could anyone improve on such a perfect vessel?

BRITOMART (7 August 1908)
No B/130 Half plate 1/200th at f13

Designed by the famous Alfred Mylne and built at Dumbarton for W. P. Burton, *Britomart* raced with the popular 52-raters along with *Creole*, *Istria*, *Bona* and *Sonia*. She was built in 1905 but did not distinguish herself until the following year when she won almost half her races. At sixty-three feet and forty-seven tons, she shows how well proportioned these old gaff-rigged cutters were compared to today's Bermudian yachts.

HISPANIA (August 1909)
No B/135/141 Half plate 1/125th at f9

One of a class of 15 metres, *Hispania* was designed by Fife of Scotland for King Alphonso XIII of Spain A keen racer, he would regularly arrive at Cowes with his royal steam yacht, the 1664-ton *Giralda*, for a season's racing against a strong fleet. The King raced frequently until racing ceased in 1914. *Hispania* is pictured here approaching the finish line off the Royal Yacht Squadron. The sailplan is clearly shown; with her three headsails, large topsail and overhanging boom she slices through the sea with her lee rail awash.

SUSANNE and CICELY (5 August 1910)
No 129 Half plate 1/120th at f9

These are two classic Fife-designed schooners built in 1904 and 1902 respectively. *Susanne*, a very pretty little ship, was only 135 tons but still raced against schooners with more than twice the tonnage, including *Germania* and *Meteor*. She was built by A. Inglis in Glasgow to a Yacht Racing Association linear rating of 79.07 but was later altered to race as a 23 metre. She was ninety-four feet long by twenty feet wide and carried 12,000 square feet of sail. In 1905 she won the Emperor's Cup, but the big cutters were becoming more popular for racing and *Susanne* spent most of her later years cruising as a luxury yacht. *Cicely*, a little larger than *Susanne* at 263 tons, won every race she entered in her first year afloat against the big schooners from Germany and Britain. She was renowned as a beautiful schooner with her classic sheerline and attractive bow.

CZARINA (1911)
No B24/A1 Half plate 1/120th at f11

Designed and built by Camper & Nicholson of Southampton for Albert Brassey, whose brother, the Lord Brassey, owned *Sunbeam*, *Cetonia* was 564 tons and 152 feet in length. She was designed for long cruises to the Baltic and Mediterranean but that did not stop her owner from entering her in the Coronation Cup for auxiliary steam vessels upwards of 340 tons. Her race was short-lived though as she ran aground. She cruised in great comfort for several thousand miles and was even fitted with a funnel able to be raised or lowered with tackle. She was commandeered by the Navy during the war and was reported torpedoed in the Bay of Biscay.

SEA FOAM (9 August 1910)
No B110 Half plate 1/150th at f11

Sea Foam, later to be renamed *La Cigale*, was built for Eugene Higgins in 1910. She was a three-masted

auxiliary topsail schooner designed and built for extended cruising by Camper & Nicholson of Southampton. At 295 tons and 122 feet overall she is only just smaller than *Sir Winston Churchill* which belongs to the Sail Training Association (299 tons and 134 feet). *Sea Foam* normally carried a permanent crew of around fifty and, as this picture shows, they knew how to trim her sails to perfection!

METEOR III (1911)
No B/114A5 Half plate 1/150th at f8

This was the third ship to bear the name *Meteor* for the German Emperor and what a magnificent sight she made! Designed and built in America to beat her owner's British cousins, she was 120 feet overall with a twenty-seven-foot beam. She was not essentially a racing yacht but a fast cruiser of 412 tons, and the Kaiser proved her to be a fast ship on home waters until she was beaten by Cecil Quentin's *Cicely*. But what a picture she makes! there is no space left to fly another sail and the crew are really busy. Just count the number of men on board and don't forget the mastheadman! She must have been travelling at over twelve knots so it was important for Frank Beken to position his rowing dinghy correctly for her approach.

ZINITA (1 August 1911)
No 60 Half plate 1/125th at f10

Zinita was one of a class of 20-raters with an overall length of fifty-two feet. She was designed by Fife of Scotland for W. S. Connell and she won, in one particularly glorious season, eighteen prizes in twenty-five starts against such hot competition as the Earl of Dunraven's *Deirdre* and Prince Henry of Battenberg's *Asphodel*. Built in 1893, she is seen here carrying three headsails and an elegant topsail with mizzen sail set. This rig proved more popular than the schooner rig and was regarded as offering the best racing to be had.

CORISANDE (4 August 1911)
No 131 Half plate 1/200th at f11

Corisande was built in 1872 by Ratsey (they were boat-builders as well as sail-makers in those days) for F. Richards. She was 150 tons and in her first four races she won three firsts and one second against her fast contemporaries *Fiona* and *Bloodhound*. This picture shows her old-fashioned straight stem and graceful stern; note also the loose footed mainsail. She was at one time owned by the Duke of York, later King George V.

WATERWITCH (1911)
No 165 Half plate 1/200th at f8

Waterwitch was designed by Fife for Cecil Whitaker and built in 1911. An elegant and powerful schooner, of 120 feet and 352 tons, she could not compete with the speed of her contemporaries and after only one season's racing, she was stripped of her masts and rigging and sent to the breakers' yard. Her owner built the 380-ton *Margherita* the next year. It was certainly a pity when one looks at the photograph showing her from windward illustrating the size and grandeur of such vessels. The rigging can clearly be seen and one wonders if a season's racing was enough time to tune a yacht to her best?

CETONIA (4 August 1911)
No 113 Half plate 1/125th at f9

Designed by J. M. Soper for the New York magnate S. M. Singer, *Cetonia* was built by Camper & Nicholson in 1902 at Southampton. She displaced 295 tons, measured 120 feet overall and carried 11,000 square feet of canvas. She was nearly rammed by the German *Meteor IV* who had not reefed in the strong wind conditions later and was out of control. This lovely craft sailed the seas for many years under the ownership of Lord Iveagh and was renowned for the sumptuous parties given aboard at Cowes by Lady Iveagh.

MARIQUITA (7 August 1911)
No 10192 Half plate 1/150th at f8

A fine start of the 19 metres, *Mariquita* leads *Octavia* and *Noroda* across the line during the Cowes Week regatta. These yachts, at 100 tons and eighty-two feet, were known as greyhounds because of their speed in light airs. Big by today's standards they were regarded as only just large enough to be respectable at that time.

PAULA (1 August 1910)
No B156 Half plate 1/150th at f11

At the turn of the century, when yachting was a fashionable sport, Frank Beken was at his busiest. Royalty regularly attended Cowes Week and the King of Spain, Alphonso XIII, raced his yacht *Hispania* against a dozen other 15-metres, among them *Paula*, seen here beating up from the west with her canvas stretched tight and sheeted well in. It was standard practice to carry a crewman at the masthead to clear the foresails when tacking – quite a job!

METEOR IV (4 August 1911)
No 114 Half plate 1/125th at f9

This fine schooner, designed by Max Oertz, was built at the Germania Yard in 1909 and at 400 tons she was the largest of the fleet to race at Cowes. This photograph was taken when her owner, the Kaiser, was aboard and *Meteor* was all set for the race across the English Channel and back. She carried full sail while her competitors were all reefed, and about two hours later the wind increased to a strength that lay her over at such an angle that she would not answer the helm and she bore away through the rest of the fleet totally out of control. She took another gust of wind which lay her over flat with her rudder half out of the water. Waves surged over her deck and through open hatches. Fortunately the wind lulled and her crew freed the sheets and she came up. Upon retiring and returning to port, she found seven feet of water below decks!

ISTRIA (10 August 1912)
No 174 Half plate 1/150th at f11

Istria was one of the popular and classic 15-metre class – originally known as the 52-raters in the Yacht Racing Association linear rating. With a tonnage of fifty-five and sixty-six feet in length, she helped in the development of the Marconi mast. Note the lacing of the topsail to the mast instead of a jackyard. These extra tall masts had to have rigging spread wider and higher, and chainplate outriggers were adopted to achieve this. The sails were of Egyptian cotton and this class was regarded as the best design within the international rating rule of the period.

WHITE HEATHER I (10 August 1912)
No 114 Half plate 1/125th at f8

White Heather was built in 1904 at Fay's Yard in Southampton for Miles B. Kennedy. Designed by Fife of Scotland, she was ninety-one feet overall and 151 tons TM. With a regular crew of twenty to handle all that canvas, our picture shows her on a dead run close to the finish line at the end of the day's racing. She rated at 82.6 and was heavily built for a racer of her day. It was becoming more

popular to adhere to Lloyd's standards and yachts were built to last. Her closest competitor was *Nyria* and the two had many a battle for first placings over the years. Is the spinnaker pole angle a mite too high?

SHAMROCK IV and *SHAMROCK III* (1914)
No 10338 Half plate 1/150th at f11

Here we see the marked difference between the older Fife-designed *Shamrock* and the later Nicholson *Shamrock IV*. She was to be matched against the American *Resolute* for the 1914 America's Cup but war broke out as she was on her way across the Atlantic and she was laid up until 1920. It was the nearest that Britain had come to winning the Cup. This was the last occasion that a time allowance system was used, successive races being on a level rating.

WESTWARD (2 August 1930)
No 15286 8" × 6" plate 1/500th at f11

Westward was probably the most famous of all the giant schooners and was one of the largest yachts to race. She was designed by the American Nat Herreshoff and built in his yard at Rhode Island in 1910. She was 135 feet overall with a waterline length of ninety-six feet. Her beam was twenty-seven feet and a draft of sixteen and a half feet. She was 323 tons and carried a massive 13,483 square feet of canvas. She was bought in 1920 by the legendary T. B. Davis. He was very fond of his new acquisition and would live on board helping with any chore when the need arose. He was so proud of her that his will followed that of George V, and his prize yacht was sunk after his death. This photograph was taken when *Westward*, in a wind strong enough for her to lower her topsails, was smoking her way to the finish line off Cowes leaving all the other schooners way behind.

OCTAVIA (1913)
No B166 Half plate 1/150th at f8

Octavia was a typical 19-metre racing gaff-rigged cutter of the early 1900s. Owned by William Burton, *Octavia* raced against other 19s, including *Mariquita* and *Corona* at regattas around the British Isles. With a Thames tonnage of 100, these craft were to be the test beds for the Marconi masts and eventual change-over to Bermudian rig. Here though, *Octavia* is obviously travelling with a fair wind behind her as she has a reef in her main.

METEOR II and AILSA (7 August 1911)
No 10212 12″ × 10″ plate 1/250th at f8

This picture shows the Fife-designed *Ailsa* crossing the bow of *Meteor II* at really close quarters. The Kaiser's second yacht was regarded as one of G. L. Watson's finest designs. A 52-rater, she was very fast, and at every regatta she was better tuned and scored increasing victories. She was designed specifically to beat the Prince of Wales' *Britannia* and first raced in Britain in 1896. It was whilst racing in the Solent that year that Baron Von Zedwitz was killed when the yacht on which he was racing, *Isolde*, was involved with *The Saint*. After a slight collision *Isolde* was carried across *Meteor*'s bows. *Meteor*'s boom scythed down the deck of *Isolde* and the crew only saved themselves by jumping overboard. The Baron was unfortunately trapped by the boom as it fell and died soon after. This picture, taken fifteen years later, shows *Meteor* on port tack about to pass safely behind *Ailsa*, a sixty-six-ton Fife cutter.

WESTWARD (2 August 1930)
No 15286 8″ × 6″ plate 1/500th at f11

See entry opposite.

QUAKER GIRL (8 August 1912)
No B195 Half plate 1/125th at f8

The big classes did not have it all their own way seventy years ago. These 32-footers with a sail area of 690 square feet were known as the 7-metre class and were extremely popular. They carried three crew and could be likened to the Dragon-class of today. K6 *Quaker Girl* was the top boat of her day. Designed by A. R. Luke and built by Luke Brothers of Hamble in 1911 she makes a fine subject as she

runs down to the next mark. Both yachts are 'gunter luff' rigged and have taken in reefs but even so the competition is tough enough for them to put up spinnakers in the strong wind. The light and shade provided by the sails and the man at the mast all make for a fine portrait of Solent racing.

NEPTUNE (3 August 1931)
No 16434 8″ × 6″ plate 1/500th at f11

Neptune was a sixty-two-ton gaff-cutter designed by the Norwegian Johan Anker. She was essentially a working cruiser from a nation of fine seamen and had come to see how she could compete against the Cowes Week yachts. She proved very successful and participated in many ocean races. This picture shows how easy it was to reef the gaff-rigged mainsail, and ease the strain on the mast with the aid of the halyard blocks and tackle. In conditions when most boats would have gone home long ago, *Neptune* could push her way through to collect class honours.

LULWORTH (1920s)
No 15801 8″ × 6″ plate 1/500th at f11

Lulworth, built for A. A. Paton, was first named *Terpsichore*, when she was designed and built in 1920 by White Brothers of Southampton. She is of 186 tons, with an overall length of ninety-five feet. She is typical of the 23-metres of the day with their huge sail area and the well fitting jackyard topsail. To look at the sails, each without a wrinkle, they look as perfect as if they were made of sheet metal. The Egyptian cotton used for sails in those days could be stretched and recut to make a perfect finished product. Her stem completes the picture of a beautiful yacht.

CANDIDA (7 August 1929)
No 11414 8″ × 6″ plate 1/500th at f11

Built for her owner, H. Andreae, in 1929, *Candida* was the first big cutter to be purpose-built with the new Bermudian rig. She was 117 feet overall with a seventy-foot waterline. With a twenty-foot beam and a draft of fourteen feet, she had a tonnage of 174 TM. She was very solidly built and was at her best in the roughest weather. In one notable race the huge schooner *Westward* retired due to high winds and *Candida* went on to win. She had in fact had a centreplate fitted to help counteract her weather helm in strong winds and had become more manageable. Her owner, one-time owner of the 19-metre *Corona*, was a first-class yachtsman and went against tradition by skippering his yacht himself.

BRITANNIA'S SAIL, RATSEY & LAPTHORN SAIL LOFT (11 April 1931)
No 16074 Half plate 1/60th and flash at f4

Messrs Ratsey and Lapthorn established their respective sail lofts at Cowes and Gosport at the end of the eighteenth century, when they already had generations of sail-making experience behind them. In fact, a Lapthorn fore topsail was worn by HMS *Victory* at the battle of Trafalgar. In 1880 the two lofts combined and proved pre-eminent throughout the golden age of yachting, all yachts of any consequence having sails made by Ratsey & Lapthorn. Yachts such as *Shamrock* and *Endeavour* carried Ratsey's sails and *Britannia*'s is pictured here in the making. In 1965 they set up their own sailcloth weaving business to cope with modern synthetic materials and were awarded the Queen's Award for export achievements in 1978. Here, twenty-five men are busy stitching and checking the Egyptian cotton of this mighty sail.

BRITANNIA (1923)
No 11747 8″ × 6″ plate 1/500th at f16

His Majesty's yacht *Britannia*, designed by G. L. Watson and built at the yard of D. & W. Henderson in 1893, is perhaps one of the most well known large yachts. She carried 10,000 square feet of sail on a mast of 110 feet, weighed 211 tons and measured 102 feet. Owned by King Edward VII, who raced her against *Satanita*, *Valkyrie* and *Calluna*, all fast yachts, she won a record thirty-three firsts out of thirty-nine starts in 1895. By 1935 she had won 200 first prizes, a record still not beaten. She was raced by King George V after the death of King Edward, and with a modern Bermudian rig, she was just as successful against her contemporaries in the J-class.

VELSHEDA (7 August 1934)
No 18917 8″ × 6″ plate 1/400th at f16

Only ten yachts were ever built as specific J-class raters although several 'big yachts' were altered to race alongside the Js. *Velsheda* was designed and built by Camper & Nicholson of Gosport in 1933 and was all of 127 feet overall with an eighty-three-foot waterline. She was not built specifically for the America's Cup but for W. L. Stephenson, Woolworth's U.K. chairman, as a European racer. She experimented with a sixty-three-foot bending boom which followed the curve of the mainsail to great effect and was an alternative to the much wider Park Avenue boom. She carried 7600 square feet of sail on a steel hull displacing 205 tons. She would race in all weathers and was a champion in her day. In 1936 she was dismasted at Plymouth along with *Endeavour II* during a weekend of gales but she had previously beaten *Britannia* in strong winds, quite an achievement as *Britannia* was reckoned to be unbeatable in strong winds. In the latter part of the 1930s the fleet was starting to wane and at the start of the war there were only four big boats racing. *Velsheda* was laid up in 1939 and until recently was on a mud berth in the Hamble river but has now been bought with a view to restoration.

YANKEE (1935)
No 19919 8″ × 6″ plate 1/500th at f16

Yankee was built in 1930 and raced with *Enterprise*, *Weetamoe* and *Whirlwind* for the honour of defending the America's Cup of that year. *Enterprise* won the trials and went on to beat *Shamrock V*, the challenger from Britain. This was the first series to be fought using J-class yachts (one of only three, the others having been fought using a handicap rating based on sail area and boat length). *Yankee* was odds-on favourite to defend in 1933, but due partly to sail and rigging failure she lost the trials to *Rainbow* who then went on to beat *Endeavour I*. In 1935 *Yankee* was bought by Gerald Lambert and she came to Cowes for a fine season's racing with the British fleet. She measured in at 228 tons TM, over a length of 126 feet, and carried 7220 square feet of sail.

SHAMROCK RUNNING BEFORE THE WIND (7 August 1934)
No 18940 8″ × 6″ plate 1/500th at f16

Shamrock was built in 1930 for Sir Thomas Lipton as a J-class yacht by Camper & Nicholson in seven months using mahogany planking on steel frames. In 1975 her latest owner brought her back home for a complete five-year refit. She was completely replanked and redecked in teak and fitted with a new aluminium mast 152′ 8″ long. She now cruises the Mediterranean in all her original splendour right down to her gold bath taps! In this picture she is running down the Solent from the west with her crew well aft keeping a steady eye on the spinnaker.

CLOSE QUARTERS (4 August 1934)
No 18852 8″ × 6″ plate 1/500th at f16

Britannia, *Astra*, *Shamrock* and *Candida* were four of the famous J-class cutters. All crews here are well aft in the stern to lift the bow and, although all appears quiet, it is deceptive as the turning buoy is approaching and it will soon be all hands to the spinnaker to bring in that huge sail and head off for the next mark. What a truly magnificent study this is, showing a perfect composition of these four giants, each one over 100 feet long and over 100 tons.

SHAMROCK DECK (1930s)
No 16179 1/500th at f16

This picture is well known, but typifies all there is to know about the J-class. It is of *Shamrock* apace, the crew in the foredeck, each one to his appointed task of handing up the flying jib (the size of a 12-metre mainsail), the man at the mast hauling slowly as each hank is attached to the forestay. Forward of him the crew is attaching the sheets, the helmsman casually keeping an eye on everything; a study of grace in the good old days.

A PEACEFUL MORNING (1926)
Half plate 1/125th at f8

Whilst the men are racing, a young boy goes off to fish and explore the River Medina. In 1926 when the world was relatively quiet, this photograph captures an especially peaceful moment. The Cowes harbour was, and still is, a fascinating area to discover and a five-mile row up the river to nearby Newport was nothing to anyone with some muscle – and maybe some bread and cheese for rations!

PART THREE

FROM AROUND 1956, hull design and international events progressed rapidly. The first challenge for the America's Cup since the war took place in 1956 with *Sceptre* representing the new class able to challenge, the 12 metre. In the next decade a series of 12 metres challenged from different countries.

We shall also see the 'Tall Ships', not only the square-rigged ships but many of the older cruising yachts being raced by the Sail Training Association, the first race being held from Brixham.

In 1959, more than fifty yachts entered for the Fastnet race, many fine yachts from America, Australia and Scandinavia. The yachts were outright racers of modern design with reverse transoms, high freeboards and of greater beam, from designers all round the world.

In this decade also, starting in 1957 we show yachts from the Admirals Cup, a series of races from Cowes, each and any country entering not more than three boats for a series of two inshore and two offshore races. These races produced the very latest designs for speed and seaworthiness, boats of light displacement, great beam and, of course, cut-throat racing.

Another race inaugurated in 1960, is the first Single-Handed Transatlantic race from Plymouth to Newport Rhode Island, U.S.A. This perpetrated many novel designs, necessitating weeks at sea, with just a single crew and producing hull forms and rigging of strength and efficiency. Also sheeting and winching were operated from the cockpit, to save movement on deck.

This decade also produced the first trimaran to sail offshore from Massachusetts to England, designed and sailed by Arthur Piver. And although multi-hulled yachts were to increase rapidly later, they were still regarded as unsafe and difficult to handle.

By 1963, more than 100 yachts were entered for the Fastnet race, providing even more compact and efficient ocean-racers, generally smaller in length, showing rod rigging and clusters of types of winches on deck for efficient and fast sail handling. Altogether it was an interesting decade, producing designs as a testbed for the next twenty years.

LATIFA (1 August 1951)
No 31396 1/500th at f16

This seventy-foot yawl, of forty-one tons, designed by Fife of Scotland for Michael Mason, had one foot in the past and one in the future, for in 1945 she raced in the Bermuda race, and in 1975 took part in the Fastnet race. She was not only designed by Fife, but also built in their boatyard, and has that magical quality of all Fife designs. Here she is racing in the Solent with a hard westerly breeze, her clean lines and powerful bow allowing her to cut through the seas without slamming into them, and her clean wake is flat enough for any critical yachtsman. The light and shade of this picture are typical of the Solent area.

TOWING OUT (1948)
No 27282 8″ × 6″ plate 1/125th at f4

Early one morning, drifting gently along with the tide on the River Medina through Cowes harbour, the trading barge *David* is towed along by a crewman. Making use of the tide and with a crew of only one or two men, these ketches carried local cargo around the coast. With their split rig and loose-footed main, they were easy to handle and would quietly ply their trade at a lazy pace to all the tiny inlets and ports around Britain.

CREOLE (4 June 1939)
No 23887 1/500th at f16

This fine schooner of 697 tons was built in Gosport by Camper & Nicholson, who also designed her. Launched in 1927 for Alex S. Cochran, she was sold soon after to Major Pope and later to Sir Conner Guthrie. She has had a varied life, being used by the Navy during the war and then sold to German owners from whom she was again bought by

Stavros Niarchos. She has now been acquired by a consortium of Danish business men and is used for training young people in the experience of going to sea, taking part in the Tall Ships races across the seas.

KIRIN (7 October 1950)
No 30607 8″ × 6″ plate 1/500th at f8

Kirin was built in 1913 by G. Lawley & Son to a design by Beavor Webb for Sir Robert Smith. She was once called *Magdalena* and was 110 feet overall at 202 tons TM. She is here seen going at fourteen knots, in a hard westerly breeze in the Solent with no flying jib or fore topsail set, but she has all the canvas she can carry. Notice the topping lift of the fore mainsail – it looks a little tight, and should be released. The helmsman must enjoy feeling the power of this ship through his fingertips on the wheel.

SCEPTRE and *EVAINE* (11 May 1958)
No 39108 8″ × 6″ plate 1/400th at f8

These two 12-metres, neck and neck, are typical of the present day challengers for the America's Cup. They are greyhounds of the sea, each year producing a more gutted-out racing shell almost totally mechanically and computer driven. Approximately seventy feet overall, *Sceptre* started anew the British challenge for the Cup which had stopped for twenty years, but she lost to the American *Columbia*.

CARIBBEE (4 August 1952)
No 32340 8″ × 6″ plate 1/500th at f11

This American yawl was built for Carlton Mitchell and was a first class all rounder in racing, cruising and on-board living. Designed as a centre-boarder by Philip Rhodes she won the SORC series in 1937, the first of three wins for him. She was 57′ 6″ overall and only drew six feet with her centre-board up on a run. Carlton Mitchell was what one might call a professional-amateur and as a first class helmsman he added many prizes to his name. Here *Caribbee* shrugs off a wave whilst tacking up the Solent coastline to the west at the start of a long Cowes Week race.

CARINA (8 August 1957)
No 38612 8″ × 6″ plate 1/400th at f11

Carina was built in Hamburg in 1955 to a Phil Rhodes design for Richard 'Tiger' Nye. He was a tough ocean racing man who sailed her many times across the Atlantic to collect a multitude of 'firsts' wherever she raced. This fifty-three-foot yawl was delivered to the States two weeks before her first race, to Sweden, which she won! In the 1955 Fastnet race (which equalled the '79 Fastnet race for rough weather) she crossed the line first as one of only twelve finishers out of forty-eight starters. Carina had cracked over fifty frames and had leaked throughout the race and 'Tiger' Nye earned his tough reputation by saying to the yachting press after the victory – though rather 'tongue in cheek' – 'now let her sink!' He was always regarded with high esteem, however, and eventually gave Carina to the U.S. Navy.

FIVE SISTERS (2 August 1959)
No 40923 8″ × 6″ plate 1/500th at f16

These are fine examples of the old Thames barges once so commonly seen around our coast during the end of the last century. Originally they carried grain, cement and other supplies to all our ports in the British Isles, usually with a crew of only two. Easily handled with an anchor always at the ready, these barges are finding it difficult to exist today. Most have been converted to private use and are sponsored or regularly chartered by big companies for conferences and entertaining. These spritsail barges are recently making a comeback thanks mainly to commercial sponsorship and hold annual races at various venues throughout the season.

CYNARA (6 August 1971)
No 54607/6 Hasselblad FP4 1/500th at f11

Forty-four years old when this photograph was taken and looking as pretty as ever, Cynara makes a fine show as she cruises past Cowes in 1971. Built in 1927 for the Marquis of Northampton and designed by C. E. Nicholson, she was used for extensive cruising all round Europe. She was a well-equipped ketch of 115 tons and she was sold later and moved to America. Recently she was bought by a Japanese syndicate to form a floating museum piece at a new marina.

BLOODHOUND (August 1962)
No 45380 1/500th at f11

From the design board of the famous Charles Nicholson, this thirty-four-ton yawl shows her paces. Built by Camper & Nicholson for Isaac Bell and launched in 1936, this 63-footer took part in most of the ocean races and proved her worth. She was purchased by Her Majesty the Queen and HRH

The Duke of Edinburgh in 1961, refitted entirely and used by the Royal household for cruising and racing over the next ten years. This picture shows His Royal Highness at the helm. She has completed thousands of miles of successful racing, and was very nearly lost in a violent storm off Selsey Bill, where she was abandoned riding at anchor close offshore. In the morning, however, she was found safe and sound still at anchor, a credit to her designer and builder.

GITANA IV (7 May 1961)
No 48265 8″ × 6″ plate 1/500th at f11

This fine auxiliary yawl of some ninety feet in length and seventy-one tons displacement, was designed and built by the Cantieri Langermani at Lavanga in 1962 for Baron Edmond de Rothschild. She was built with comfort in mind and to this day is still in demand as a luxury charter vessel in the West Indies. Our picture shows her at the start of a cross channel race to France and in the stiff breeze she has 'her ear to the sea' and, with her mizzen stowed to ease weather helm, her crew are making ready for the next tack to take her through to the Needles channel into open water.

NORYEMA IV (2 August 1965)
No 49539 8″ × 6″ plate 1/500th at f11

Noryema was owned by Englishman Ron Amey who later went on to be the only foreigner to win the Bermuda race. Here we see him with his fourth yacht. She was a sloop of seventeen tons TM with a length of forty-five feet overall on a thirty-three feet waterline and was designed and built by Camper & Nicholson of Southampton in 1965. This picture shows her crew suffering in squally conditions 'riding the weather rail'. This practice was deemed unsafe by the Royal Ocean Racing Club and has since been banned.

VAMP OF HAMBLE (1 August 1966)
No 50791 8″ × 6″ plate 1/500th at f8

A classic portrayal of a yacht in action! This eleven-ton Tyler-built ocean racer of thirty-eight feet heels over taking a gust from the south-west on her beam. Designed by Alan Buchanan and launched in 1966 she is made of the now popular glass reinforced plastic and she rates at 23.7 feet. Vamp is fast approaching the end of her run and holds her spinnaker up to the buoy. Her foredeck crew are busy raising the jib prior to lowering the spinnaker. She is well reefed and one crewman valiantly leans on the boom (thinking that his light weight might stop the boom crashing over if she gybed in a roll!); but notice the lady helmsman has the tiller amidships just proving how well balanced the yacht is.

CAPRICE OF HUON (25 July 1965)
No 49429 8″ × 6″ glass plate 1/500th at f11

Caprice was built in Tasmania in 1951 to a Robert Clark design and was successfully raced in Australian waters by her owner, Gordon Wingate. In 1965 she sailed all the way to Cowes to represent Australia in her first challenge for the Admiral's Cup. Although well placed with her two other compatriots, it was not until the following challenge in 1967 that the team was successful in winning the prized trophy. By then Caprice was sixteen years old so it was no mean feat! She is shown here with the minimum amount of crew on deck well aft surfing her way eastwards up the Solent in a typical wind against tide swell.

ROUNDABOUT (21 May 1967)
No 51268 1/500th at f16

Designed by Sparkman & Stephens of the USA of whom Herman Frers made a large part of the design structure, Roundabout was the first one-tonner to be built in England. She was built at Cowes by the firm of Lallow, in 1966, a few weeks before the first one-ton races in Denmark, the first of which she won. She was one of the more successful yachts of her owner, Sir Max Aitken. She won the famous Round the Island race from Cowes, in two consecutive years, and also the Queen's Cup in 1967. Her crew are seen here sitting out on trapezes, a practice which was stopped by the Royal Ocean Racing Club very soon after, as it was considered unsafe with possible loss of crew in an ocean race. When partaking in the single-handed Transatlantic race, she blew up and sank, believed to be the result of a Calor Gas bottle below, but her crewman was picked up none the worse for wear. Her sister yacht Clarionet, built immediately after Roundabout, with a slightly different design, was another successful one-tonner.

VAE VECTIS (8 August 1964)
No 48489 8″ × 6″ plate 1/400th at f16

A powerful shot of the start of the Yarmouth to Santander race at the end of Cowes Week 1964. *Vae Vectis* is in a commanding position well reefed to weather of *Janessa* and *Sandettie*. She was built to Lloyd's 100A1 standard for Mr K. Trent by the yard of E. W. Sutton to a design by Alan Buchanan and launched in 1961. She was just over thirty-two feet in length and rated at 23.33 for RORC races. Every two years (the 'odd' years), Cowes Week ends with the famous Fastnet race, around the south coast of Ireland. In the 'even' years, a long distance race is also held and in 1964 it was from Yarmouth to Santander in Spain, a distance of 500 miles. Even in the sheltered waters of the Solent, these yachts are experiencing a strong running sea, only a foretaste of what is to follow once outside the Needles channel and into open sea!

IOLAIRE (9 August 1975)
No 55354/6 Hasselblad FP4 1/500th at f8

A classic yawl built by Harris Bros in 1905 and seventy years old when this photograph was taken of her competing in the Fastnet race of 1975! Originally a single-masted gaff-rigged cutter, she made her name as a very fast cruiser racer and, after several refits and complete rig change, she languishes in the Caribbean where her owner, Don Street, writes books on Caribbean cruising. *Iolaire* is forty-four feet long, with a seven-foot beam and carries 1100 square feet of sail.

BAMBI II (9 July 1965)
No 49377 8″ × 6″ plate 1/500th at f11

Bambi was a little Class Three ocean racer owned by Frenchman Andre Ple in 1965. This ten-tonner TM comes from St Malo and was a regular competitor in races in Britain. Built by Halmatic to a Camper & Nicholson design in glass reinforced plastic she was thirty-two feet long rated at 21.24. Here she is fast catching the Class Two yachts with some nasty clouds approaching from the south. Catching the breeze on a nice run she surfs on her way through the Solent on a cross channel race to Dinard in France.

LORD JIM (1971)
No 55886/11 Hasselblad FP4 1/500th at f11

Built in Neponset, Massachusetts as the *Meridian* by Lawley & Sons in 1936, *Lord Jim* was designed by John Alden as a schooner. Around seventy feet long with a beam of fifteen feet she sets 2400 square feet of sail. She spent most of her life in the Caribbean and when last seen in 1978 was starting a world cruise. For several years she was a popular charter vessel working out of Antigua and here she is racing during Antigua Sailing Week. Her lovely teak decks and bright varnish glitter in the sun and her skipper and crew are justifiably proud to sail her.

ORYX (3 August 1966)
No 50831 8″ × 6″ plate 1/500th at f8

What a Cowes Week 1966 was. Here is *Oryx* battling through a force nine towards the finish line and home. She is a forty-five-foot cutter designed by the late John Illingworth and Angus Primrose (lost overboard in Autumn 1980). *Oryx* was built for Frenchman Francis Bouygues, and she proved one of their most successful designs, competing in the ill-fated 1979 Fastnet. She seems to be coping here quite well with only a small reef in her main and, although her lee rail was awash, she never once buried her bow.

GORCH FOCK (20 June 1966)
No 50490 8″ × 6″ plate 1/500th at f16

This is the second ship to carry the name *Gorch Fock*. Belonging to the West German Navy she serves as a training ship for around 200 cadets on each cruise. Designed and built in Hamburg by Blohm & Voss she is a three-masted barque launched in 1958. She is almost 266 feet long with a beam of thirty-nine feet and a tonnage of 1727 TM. With her regular crew of sixty-nine, she has participated in almost every Tall Ships race and has more 'firsts' than any other ship in

her class. These classic square riggers are sadly few and far between and always cause a stir whenever they call. Fortunately their popularity has recently increased thus giving young trainees a sample of real 'sailing before the mast'.

AMPHITRITE (28 September 1967)
No 51971 8″ × 6″ plate 1/500th at f16

This three-masted barquentine was built in 1887 for Colonel MacGregor by Camper & Nicholson and she is still afloat today, under German ownership and used as a sail training ship for cadets. She is 100 feet overall and displaces 161 tons. Her main and mizzen are fore and aft rigged and her foremast is fully rigged including a square forecourse. Her design graduated from the Trafalgar ships era and, with her clipper bow and counter, she is typical of yachts of her period. When this photograph was taken she was eighty years old and under French ownership. With a mistral wind howling through her rigging, men are being sent aloft to shorten sail even further.

LAMADINE (1967)
No 51251 1/500th at f16

This ninety-eight-ton yawl was launched in 1967 and built for Jack Frye. She is of wood composite construction, of double diagonal mahogany. She has an unusual deck consisting of double skin plywood, with a foam-filled sandwich and a teak deck laid above. Designed by Laurent Giles, and built at Camper & Nicholson's yard at Southampton, she is shown here on her first trials, the very essence of a modern cruising yawl. She carries the most modern equipment below and is equipped to sail all the seas of the world.

PART FOUR

By 1970, yachts will now be seen to be built of other materials than wood. Glass reinforced plastic had made its mark some years ago, but now big yachts of sixty to eighty feet were being built on a production line, of great strength and durability, able to race and cruise around the world. In 1971 the Fastnet was raced with more than one hundred yachts entered, the winner being *Ragamuffin* from Australia. A record of over 300 yachts entered for the 1979 Fastnet race. In the next two decades we shall see yachts racing round the world regularly; the first race was held in 1973 with fifteen entering, and won by a sixty-five-foot glass fibre yacht *Sayula* with an average speed of 7.41 knots.

Radical mono-hulled yachts and radical multi-hulled designs were racing across the Atlantic, the Pacific and round the world. *Pen Duick IV* of unusual trimaran design, seventy feet overall, crossed the Atlantic in record time of twenty-one days and thirteen hours. Alain Colas also sailed her round the world single-handed but lost his life when sailing her across the Atlantic a few years later. Neither man or craft were found.

Single-handed yachts will be seen to have greatly increased in size, a notable example being *Vendredi XIII*, 128 feet in length, which raced across the Atlantic in 1972 and was second to arrive.

Later in 1976 an even bigger schooner, four-masted and of 245 tons and over 230 feet long, by name *Club Mediterranée* also raced across single-handed complete with satellite navigation equipment.

Now in the 1980s – from the testbeds of the Admirals Cup challengers, the out and out racing machines – will be seen our finest ocean-racers and cruisers. With their scientifically designed hull forms, their superbly cut sails, their 'coffee grinder' winches, their rod rigging, these yachts are the thoroughbreds of today – the 'Maxi' yachts of eighty and ninety feet, the 'two tonners', the 'one tonners', etc.

So, glass reinforced plastic replaces teak and oak, Dacron replaces Egyptian cotton, Terylene and other manmade fibres replace manila and hemp sheets. Variable cut spinnakers, 'bigboys' and 'tallboys', feather-light genoas made from 'Mylar', a new plastic film, and carbon filament materials for masts are now the order of the day. The world is now our oyster; it is symbolical perhaps that the 185 ton three-masted schooner *Atlantic*, which has held the record for the fastest Atlantic crossing from America to England since 1905, has in 1980 been beaten by Eric Tabarly in his revolutionary trimaran *Paul Ricard*, by nearly two days – the record now stands at ten days and five and a half hours.

DIANA II (2 August 1971)
No 54560/9 Hasselblad FP4 1/500th at f8

All hands to the spinnaker to gather in this huge sail and replace it with the genoa. In a freshening breeze, *Diana II* battles her way on through the rising seas in the Cowes regatta of 1971. This is where teamwork counts. Three men are gathering in the sail while one waits with the sailbag to whip it away below for repacking ready for the next run. *Diana II*, a sixty-foot sloop, was originally built in 1935 and extensively refitted in 1963. Her solid build and teak decks looking a little old-fashioned today, she still shows lighter boats how to race in heavy weather!

WINSOME (1970)
Hasselblad FP4 1/500th at f16

Winsome is a Nicholson forty-three-foot hull, bought by David May of the Berthon Boat Co. and completed by his company. She is of glass reinforced plastic, with a teak deck and has been fitted out most elegantly. She is an extremely good sea boat with an elegant interior and exterior finish. In her first season she obtained twenty-three first prizes, racing in the hardest of weather. Here she is seen recovering from a temporary 'knock down' in the squalls that occur in our hard westerly winds in the Solent.

ROYALIST (6 July 1971)
No 54618/9 Hasselblad FP4 1/500th at f8

This ship was built by Groves & Guttridge of Cowes for the sea cadets in 1971 to a design by Colin Mudie. A very pretty little brig, she was constructed of steel and has a tonnage of 110. She is seventy-six and a half feet overall with a beam of nineteen and a half feet and a draft of nine feet. Designed on the lines of the old brig HMS *Martin*, she was awarded

the Lloyd's Register Yacht award in 1971 for the best designed and equipped vessel for its purpose. She carries a crew of thirty-two with twenty-four of those being cadets under training on seven-day cruises. She sails all round the British Isles and competes in Sail Training races both here and abroad. She is painted after the style of a Blackwall frigate and under full sail has reached speeds over twelve knots.

SAYULA II (1973)
No 54941/5 Hasselblad FP4 1/500th at f8

Sayula was a sixty-four-foot ketch built by Nautor of Finland to a Sparkman & Stephens design. She entered the first fully crewed Round the World race in 1973 and came first on handicap. A production Swan 65-class built of glass reinforced plastic, her crew had not expected to win at all and enjoyed a pleasant cruise. Here she is at the start of the Fastnet race of 1973. The wind pushing her hard, she is heavily reefed and the crew are high on the weather rail.

GINSPINNER (2 August 1975)
No 55306/11 Hasselblad FP4 1/500th at f11

The spinner class, of which *Ginspinner* is a good example, had the difficult task of surviving through the transition from the RORC to the IOR measurement rules. Designed by Michael Henderson in 1966, they were eligible to race in the Junior Offshore Group rating at eighteen feet, then in the new half-ton cup. With their twenty-four-foot waterline they were eligible to race in RORC where they rated at nineteen feet. *Ginspinner* and her glass reinforced plastic sisterships competed in numerous races where they raced *Pas avec la gloire mais pas sans honneur*. *Ginspinner* is captured here beating in close quarters with *Rock'N'Goose* on their way to the first mark in a Solent JOG race. She measured twenty-eight feet overall with a beam of 9′ 9″ displacing three tons carrying 350 square feet of sail. The class was designed with an internal layout complementary to both cruising and offshore racing and, as can be seen from the photograph, they proved exciting to handle – even if the helmsman and foredeck crew appear a little pensive!

PENDUICK VI (10 August 1974)
No 55145/9 Hasselblad FP4 1/500th at f8

This ketch was designed by French architect André Mauric, and was constructed at Brest. She was raced by the famous French helmsman, Eric Tabarly, and in the Round the World race of 1978 she twice lost her mast in mid-ocean (South Atlantic and Pacific). Tabarly won the 1976 single-handed Transatlantic race in this yacht after steering many days and nights after the auto-steering had broken. This picture shows her fully crewed for the 1974 Coronation Bowl race with a good strong breeze right on the nose. At thirty-four tons TM she is seventy-two feet long.

FLICA II (1971)
No 55879/11 Hasselblad FP4 1/500th at f11

Now converted to a cruising ketch, *Flica II* was once a fast racing 12-metre. Built in 1939 by Fife of Scotland to a Laurent Giles design, she was sixty-seven feet long with a waterline of forty-six and a half feet, a beam of twelve feet and a tonnage TM of thirty-four. Our photograph shows how she looks now with a deckhouse and cut-down rig. Still fast, she proved popular with charterers in the Caribbean as they could visit more islands in the time allowed! Here she is competing in Antigua Race Week where all manner of yachts compete in cruising and racing classes under the scorching hot sun and where the après-sail of barbecues and rum on the beaches to the sound of steel bands is a sheer delight!

VENDREDI TREIZE (7 June 1972)
No 54701 Hasselblad FP4 1/500th at f11

Vendredi Treize was designed by Dick Carter of the USA and was a one-off for the single-handed Transatlantic race. Of thirty-five tons and 128 feet overall, she had a sailplan of three boomed genoas set on three masts. Sailed by Frenchman Yves Terlain, she came second in the race of 1972 and if she had not been unlucky with the wind she would have won. Built of aluminium, she is technically a staysail schooner but proved rather under-canvased for her size. She has raced since but could not hold her own against the speedy trimarans and she was dwarfed by the even larger French entry in 1976, the 236-foot four-masted *Club Méditerranée*. They both now reside in the Caribbean available for charter and making a striking sight wherever they call.

PENDUICK IV (17 June 1972)
No 54706/6 Hasselblad FP4 1/500th at f11

This ultra-modern trimaran looked more like a machine than a yacht, but she certainly moved fast! An aluminium ketch of sixty-five feet she raced from Los Angeles to Hawaii, a distance of some 2225 miles, in eight and a half days at an average speed of 10.8 knots. She also won the single-handed Transatlantic race for Eric Tabarly in 1972 in a record twenty-one and a half days. Later she was known to have reached twenty knots on her Round the World sail when skippered by Alain Colas. Sadly, both he and this yacht disappeared during the Route de Rhum race from St Malo to the West Indies in November 1978. On looking at the rig of this racing machine it seems a wonder that one man can manage her – once a multihull of this size turns over it is usually the end.

RENDEZ-VOUS (6 August 1971)
No 54599/12 Hasselblad FP4 1/500th at f8

Rendez-Vous ex Rubin was racing for Sweden during the Admiral's Cup series of 1971 when this photograph was taken. Running down the Solent with a stiff sou'westerly behind her, she took a knockdown and broached round 180 degrees to windward. With her jib, main and spinnaker all aback she came hurtling towards our photographic launch. Making our escape we managed to shoot 'over the shoulder' and capture the sight on film. She turned head to wind and with a great thunderclap her spinnaker filled again and she was off again to rejoin the fleet with water pouring from her decks!

KIALOA III (9 August 1975)
No 55356/8 Hasselblad FP4 1/500th at f11

Designed by Mr Pendrick of Sparkman & Stephens, *Kialoa* was launched at the yard of Palmer Johnson in 1974. Built of aluminium she displaces nearly forty tons on a hull seventy-nine feet by a seventeen and a half feet beam. Her sail area is over 9000 square feet with a giant spinnaker of over 5000 square feet. John Kilroy has led her to victory in many a race in her worldly travels, amongst them three Fastnets. *Kialoa* was world ocean racing champion in 1975, '76 and '77 having competed and getting line honours in countless ocean races, his most memorable being the Fastnet in 1975 and the Sydney–Hobart in 1977. Our photograph here was taken during that Fastnet when *Kialoa* was swift to show a clean pair of heels to her class mates and quickly overtook the earlier starters. Her rig was recently altered and she now sails with a single mast which solved one problem; competitors used to think she was two yachts sailing in close company when viewed from a distance as her mizzen was so tall!

THUNDER (22 September 1973)
No 54989/1 Hasselblad FP4 1/500th at f8

A spectacular shot into the sun of a fine cruiser racer. *Thunder* was a Sparkman & Stephens designed Contessa 38 from the Lymington yard of Jeremy Rodgers. Built of glass reinforced plastic she was a one-tonner rating at 27.5, distinguishing herself at the One-Ton Cup in Sardinia in 1973. She was also the most successful one-tonner in the Solent Points series and other south coast of England events. This design, now superseded by the Contessa 35s, was well appointed below and offered excellent sport for the racing man who also wanted a cruising boat. Here she runs before the wind with all three sails pulling well. The lighting through the sails and on the waves sets the scene.

DAR POMORZA (4 August 1974)
No 55101/4 Hasselblad FP4 1/500th at f5.6

A tremendous sight in 1974 when a fleet of international Tall Ships was reviewed by HRH The Duke of Edinburgh on board *Britannia* during Cowes Week. The Solent was packed with small craft of every description and *Dar Pomorza* here moves up for the salute with her men at attention lining the decks. *Dar Pomorza* is the oldest full-rigged training vessel afloat today, having been built in 1909 by the Blohm & Voss yard at Hamburg. Originally named *Prinzess Eitel Friedrich* and owned by the German Merchant Navy, she was handed to the French after the First World War but she was sold to the Polish State Sea School in 1929. She is built of steel and measures 226½ feet overall with a beam of forty-one feet. She carries 20,450 square feet of canvas and with a crew of thirty she trains 150 cadets.

TOVARICH (2 May 1976)
No 55433/10 Hasselblad FP4 1/500th at f11

Tovarich was launched in 1933 as the first of a trio of Tall Ships built for the German Navy between the wars. She was built at the yard of Blohm & Voss who also designed her and she was originally named *Gorch Fock*. Measuring nearly 204 feet overall with a beam of nearly forty feet she displaces 1727 tons TM and she carries 135 cadets and eighty-five officers. She was pressed into war service but was sunk off Stralsund in 1945 to be salvaged by the Russians three years later. After extensive renovations she was renamed *Tovarich II* in 1953 and has competed regularly in Sail Training events since then. In this photograph she is on her way to meet her sister ships the *Eagle* and the *Sagres* in New York.

SIR WINSTON CHURCHILL (1976)
No 55432/5 Hasselblad FP4 1/500th at f11

This fine three-masted topsail schooner was designed specifically for the British Sail Training Association for training young cadets and was launched in 1966. She was built by Richard Dunston Co. of Hull to a Camper & Nicholson design and is constructed of steel. She is almost 138 feet overall with a beam of twenty-five feet displacing 299 tons TM. She and her sister ship, *Malcolm Miller*, each carry thirty-nine cadets on two-week cruises throughout the year. In this particular photograph, *Sir Winston Churchill* was crewed entirely by girls on their way to New York from Plymouth to take part in America's bicentenary celebrations. She cuts a fine sight here twenty miles out into the English Channel with her canvas stretched to the limit creaming along 'with a bone in her teeth'!

YEOMAN XXI (5 August 1980)
No 26427 Hasselblad Ektachrome 64 1/500th at f8

It is only 10.35 am and twenty Class One yachts cross the Royal Yacht Squadron start line for the Britannia Cup race during Cowes Week. Amongst them is *Yeoman XXI* with her owners Owen & Robin Aisher on board. Chartered to HRH Prince Philip when he competes in the Cowes regatta, *Yeoman* has been a regular sight since her launch in 1978. She is a Peterson design built and fitted out by Martland Marine and Rank Marine International using aluminium. At forty-six feet overall she rates for racing at 36.1 and even with a reefed main she makes good speed through the choppy seas and the stiff sou'westerly! Incidentally we were getting just as wet in our photographic launch!